animals

Who does what?

Published in 2002 by Brockhampton Press
20 Bloomsbury Street
London WC1B 3JH
a member of the Caxton Publishing Group

© 2002 Brockhampton Press

Designed and produced for Brockhampton Press
by Open Door Limited
Langham, Rutland

Title: animals: who does what?
ISBN: 1 84186 085 9
Printed in Indonesia by TK Printing

animals

Who does what?

BROCKHAMPTON PRESS

Who lives on a farm?

If you go to a farm, you might see these animals.

cow

sheep

goat

horse

pig

hen

Who says mooo?

Can you make the sounds these farm animals make?

oink oink

cock-a-doodle-do

neighh

moOO

quack quack

baaa

Who lives at home?

All these animals make good pets. Do you have a pet in your home?

hamster

rabbits

dog

guinea pig

goldfish

kitten

Who lives in the garden?

All these animals live outside.
How many have you seen in
your garden?

frog

bumble bee

snail

worm

bird

hedgehog

Who lives in the sea?

All these animals live in the sea.
Do you know what they are?

shark

seahorse

fish

dolphin

starfish

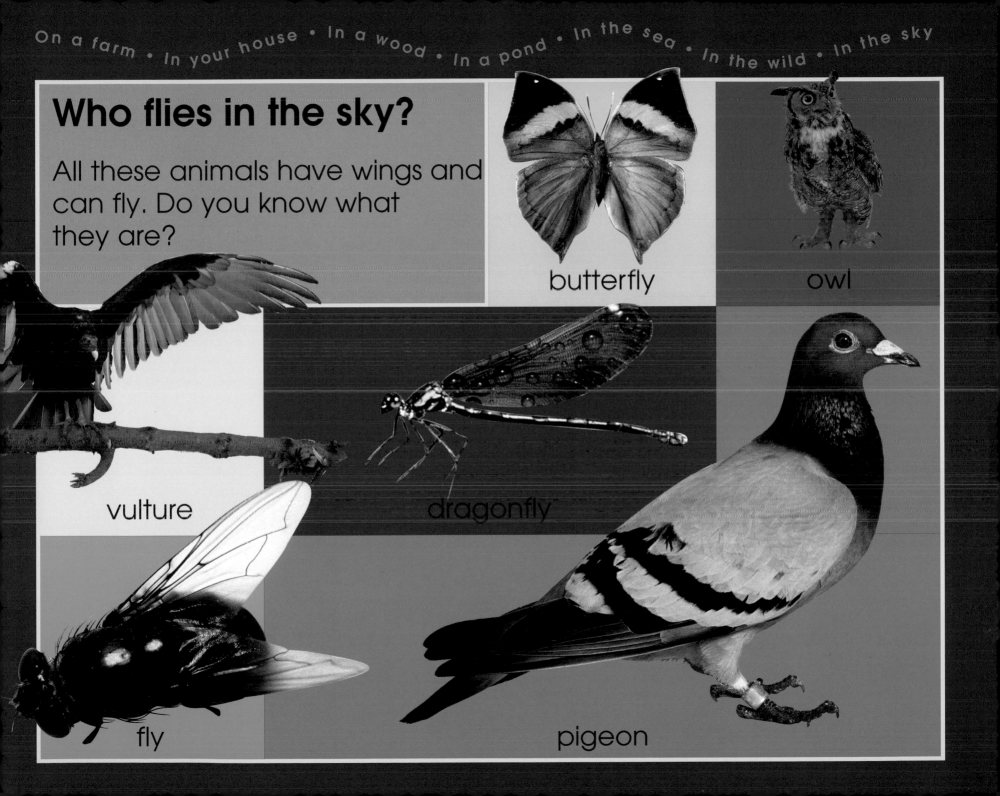

Who flies in the sky?

All these animals have wings and can fly. Do you know what they are?

butterfly

owl

vulture

dragonfly

fly

pigeon

Who does what?

All these animals make different noises. Do you know what they are?

rribbit rribbit

roar

hissssssss

meeeoow

woof woof

chirp chirp chirp chirp chirp chirp chirp

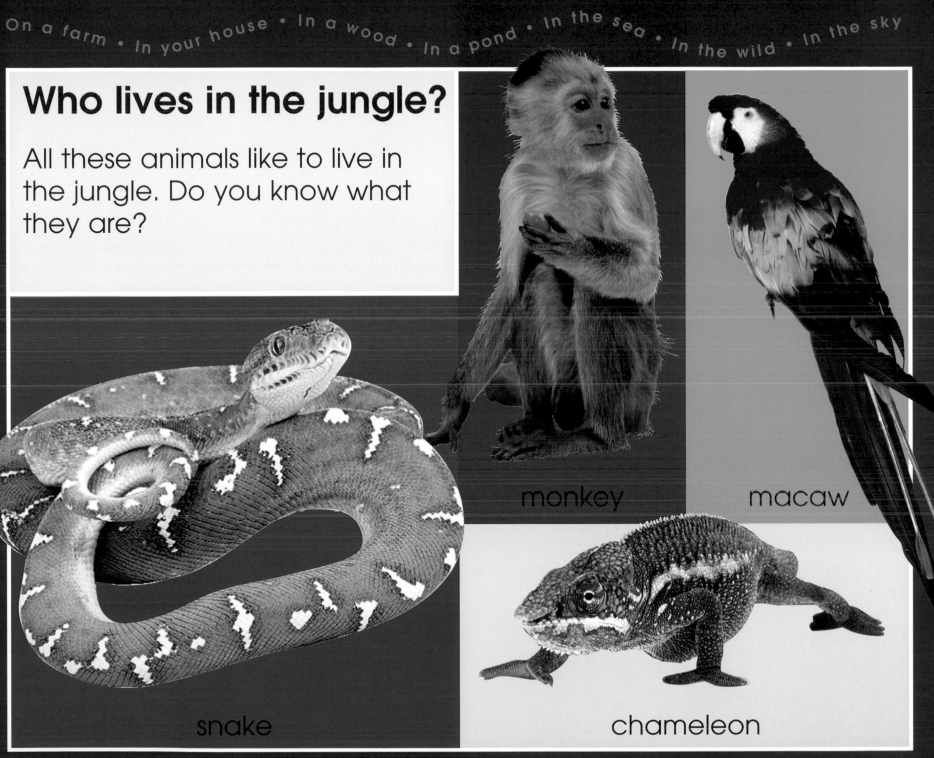

Who lives in the jungle?

All these animals like to live in the jungle. Do you know what they are?

monkey

macaw

snake

chameleon

What bird is that?

All of these animals are very
different, but they are all birds.
Do you know their names?

toucan

pelican

turkey

eagle

puffin

owl

penguin

Who can jump?

All these animals jump and hop as they move around. Do you know what they are?

toad

kangaroo

grasshopper

frog

rabbits

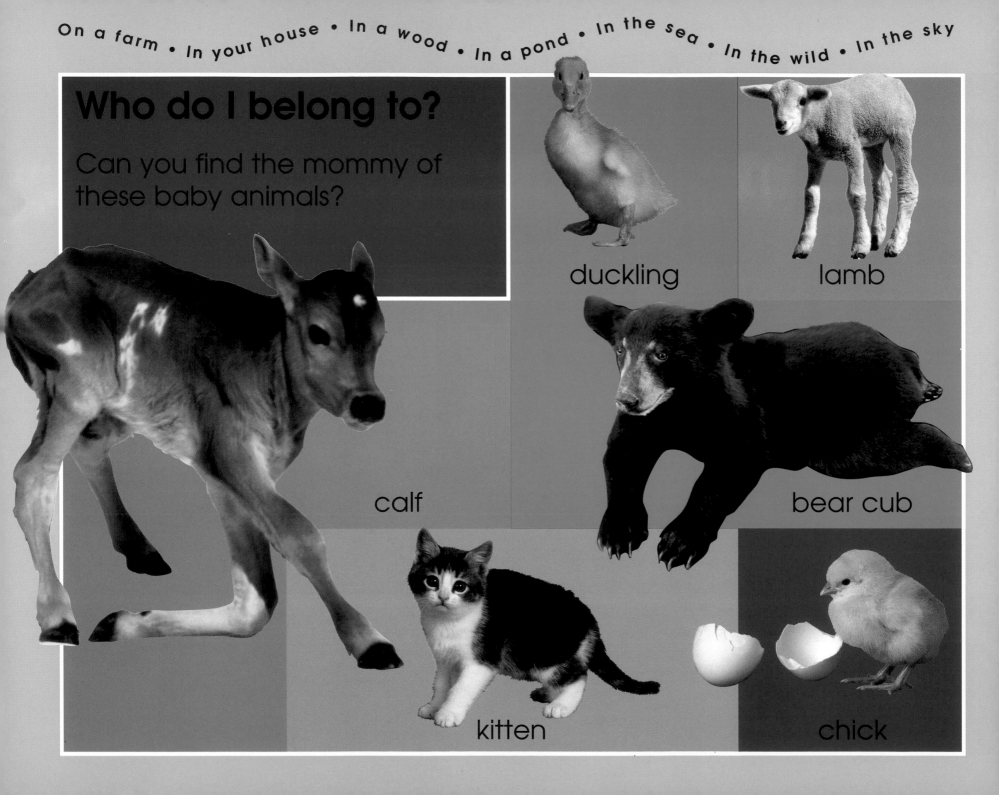

Who do I belong to?

Can you find the mommy of these baby animals?

duckling

lamb

calf

bear cub

kitten

chick

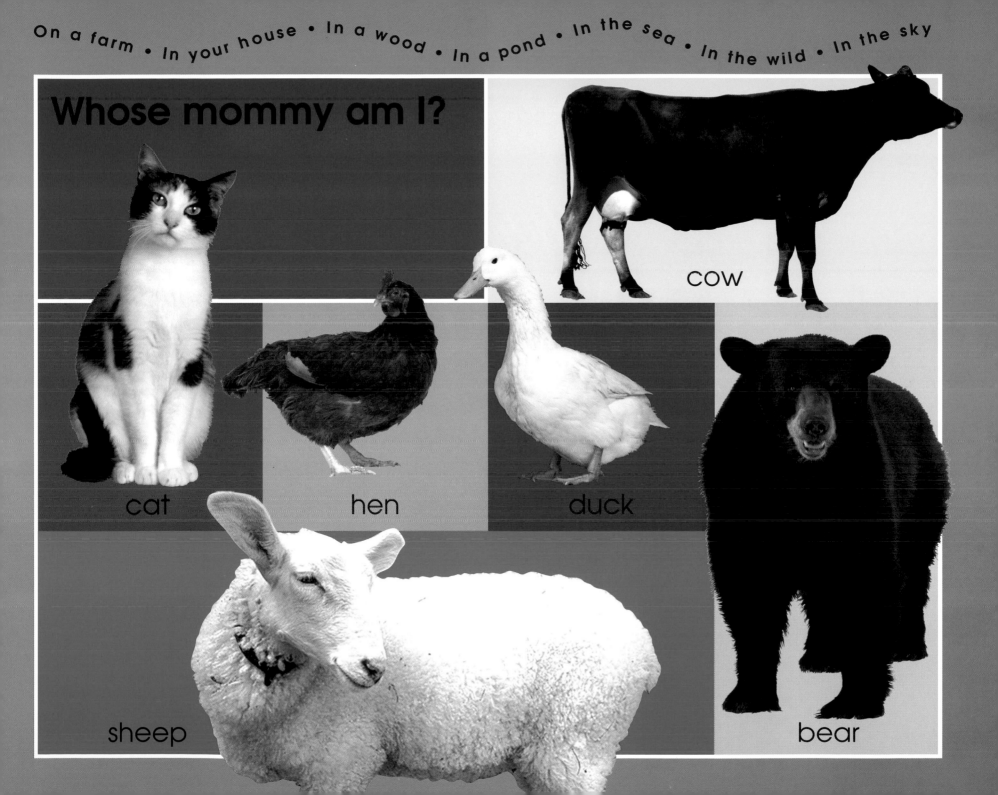

Whose mommy am I?

cow

cat

hen

duck

bear

sheep

Spots and stripes!

Can you match the patterns with the animals opposite?

stripes

spots

stripes

stripes

spots

spots

stripes

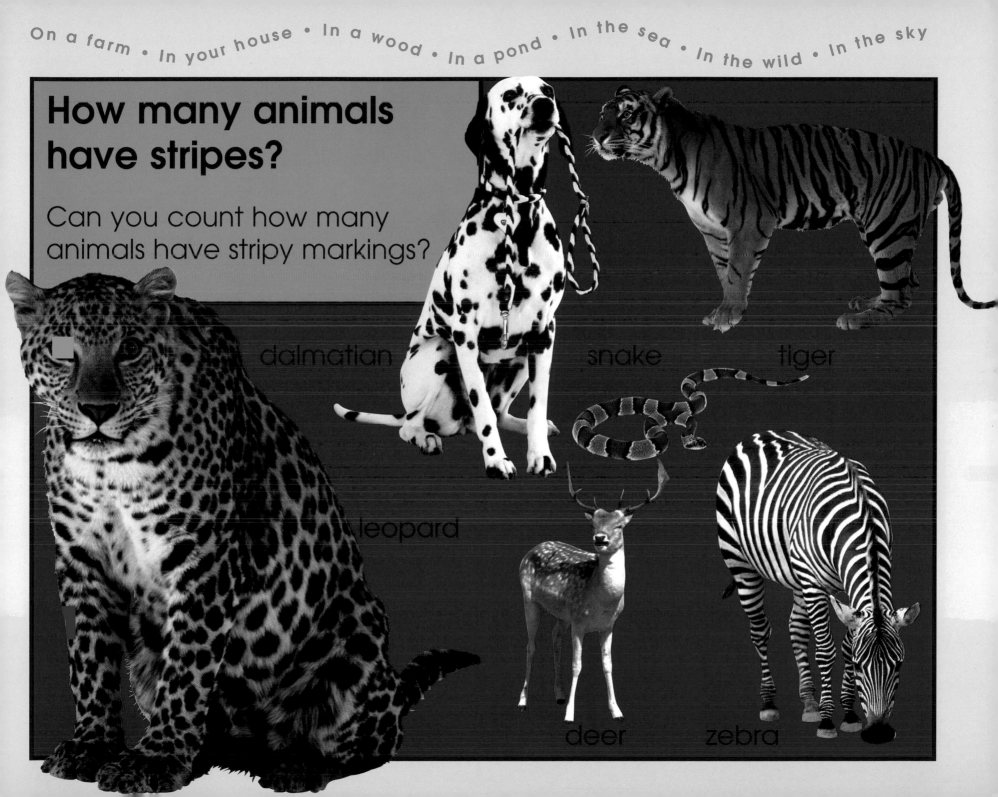

How many animals have stripes?

Can you count how many animals have stripy markings?

dalmatian

snake

tiger

leopard

deer

zebra

Skin and scales!

All of these animals have leathery skin or scales covering their bodies. Do you know their names?

elephant

fish

lizard

crocodile

snake

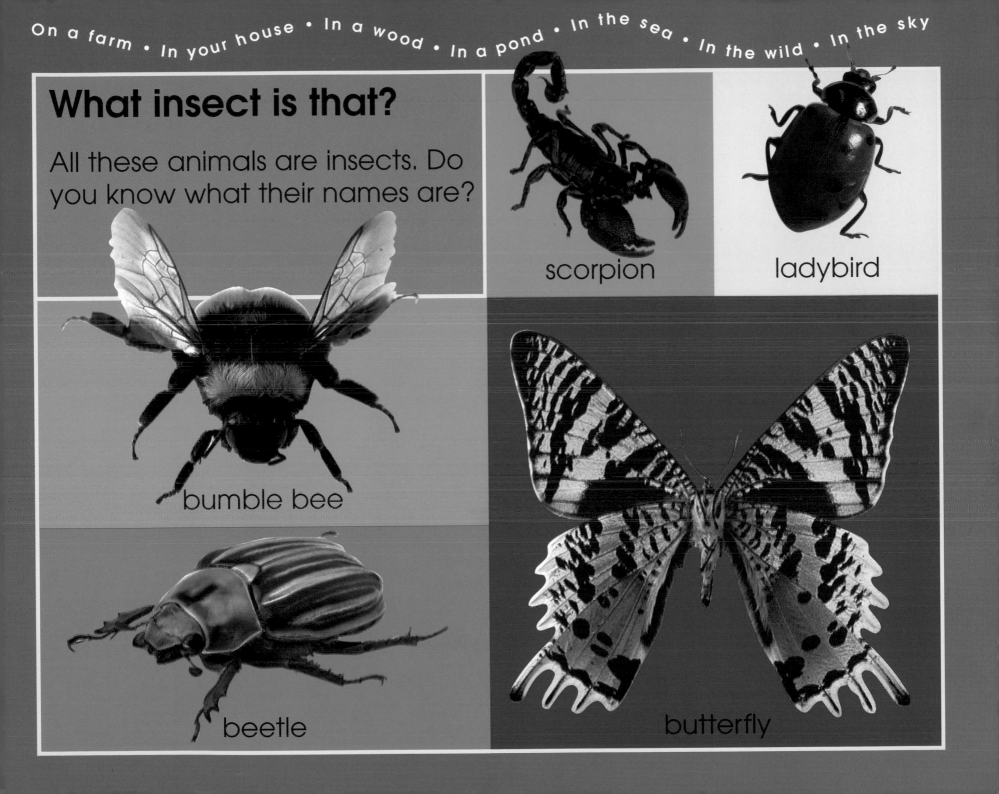

What insect is that?

All these animals are insects. Do you know what their names are?

scorpion

ladybird

bumble bee

beetle

butterfly

Who is the biggest?

All these animals are very big, but who has the longest neck? Who has the largest ears? And who has the biggest feet?

bison

giraffe

elephant

Who is the smallest?

All these animals are very small.
Who likes to run around a wheel?
And who likes to eat cheese?

kittens

bird

hamster

rat

mouse

ducklings

puppy

Who lives in a shell?

All these animals carry their homes around on their backs. Do you know what they are?

turtle

hermit crab

snail

tortoise

Who likes the water?

All these animals can swim and like to live near water, in a pond or river. Do you know what they are?

beaver

frog

duck

swan

crocodile

Fur and feathers!

Can you match the colors
and patterns with the
animals opposite?

fur

fur

fur

feathers

feathers

feathers

feathers

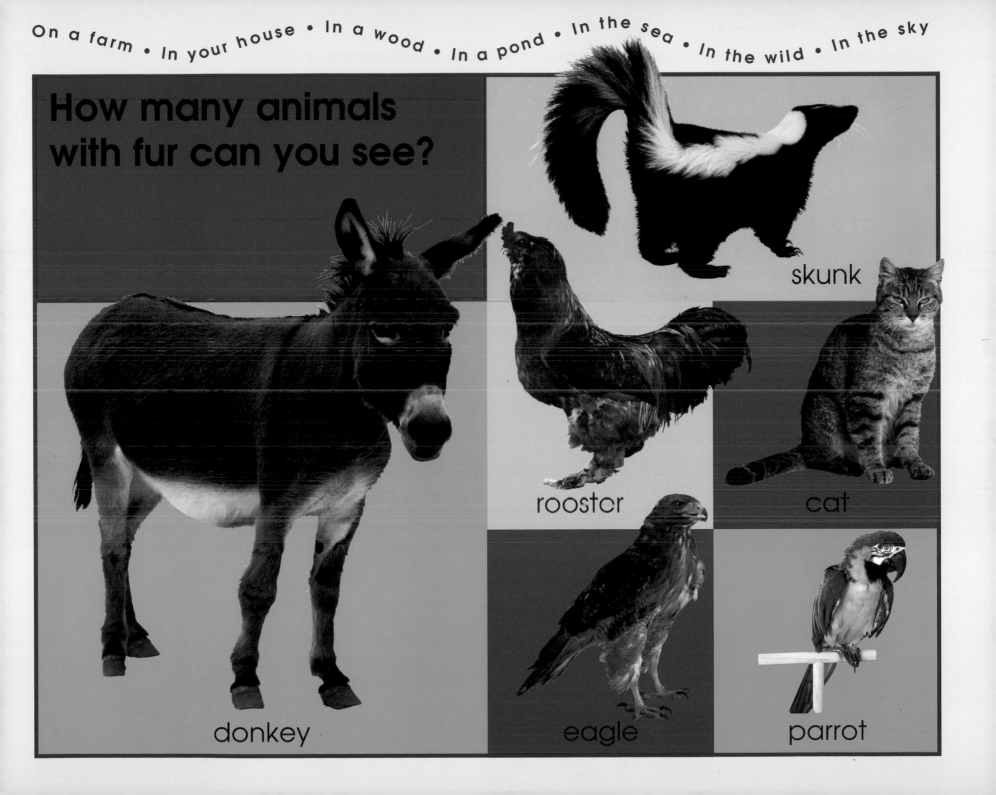

How many animals with fur can you see?

skunk

rooster

cat

donkey

eagle

parrot

Wild animals!

Here are even more wild animals. Do you know what they are?

camel

chimp

vulture

chinchilla

panda

Who does what?

Can you make a sound like these animals?

grrrow!

howwl

squawk

eeee-aw

Who likes the cold?

These animals all live happily in places where there is lots of snow and ice. Do you know what they are?

seal

penguins

polar bears

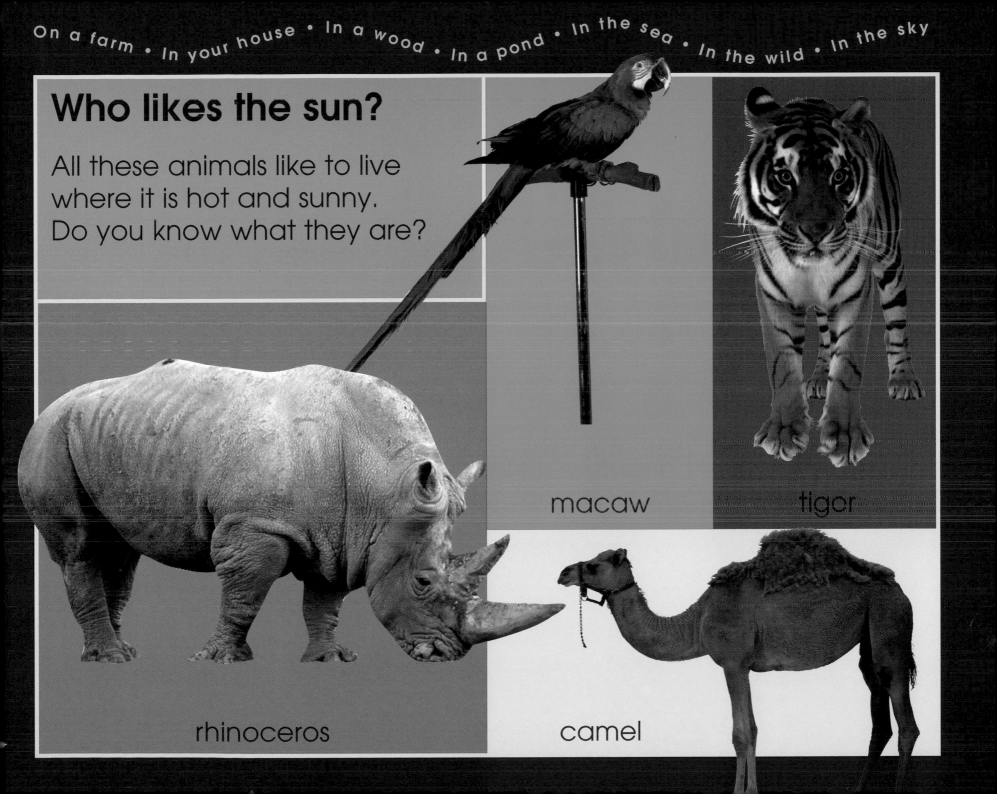

Who likes the sun?

All these animals like to live where it is hot and sunny. Do you know what they are?

macaw

tiger

rhinoceros

camel

What can you see?

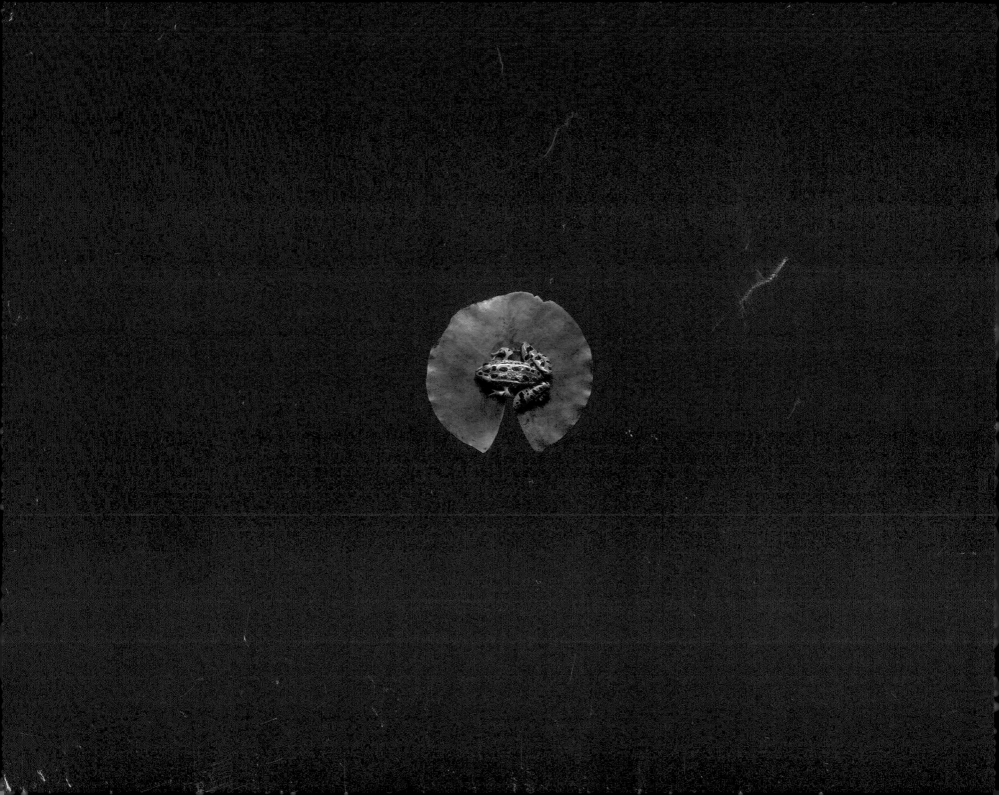